Pure WORDS

IDENTIFYING THE KING JAMES BIBLE AS GOD'S PURE WORDS IN ENGLISH.

JEFFERY DRAKE JR.

Pure WORDS

IDENTIFYING THE KING JAMES BIBLE AS GOD'S PURE WORDS IN ENGLISH

ISBN: 978-1-961110-32-8

Library of Congress Cataloguing-in-Publication Data: LCCN: Pending

Trust House Publishers, Inc.
220 Paseo del Pueblo Norte
P.O. Box 3181
Taos, NM USA 87571
www.TrustHousePublishers.com

Ordering Information: Special discounts are available on quantity purchases by churches, associations, and U.S. trade bookstores and wholesalers. For details, contact the publisher at the address above or at our toll-free number: 1-844-321-4202.

Cover design by Trust House Publishers, Inc.

Interior layout by Ye Olde Typesetter, Show Low, Arizona USA

Illustrations by Adobe Stock.

4 5 6 7 8 9 10 11 12

TABLE OF CONTENTS

Introduction

The purpose of this small book is to inform Christians who are currently not using a King James Bible, why they should be. The other purpose of this book is to encourage and strengthen Christians who are using the King James Bible, to be strong, steadfast, and confident that the King James Bible is in fact God's pure words in English.

The claim that the KJB is too difficult for common people in the 21st century to understand is deception, and simply not true. The KJB uses a few words that are not used often outside of the Bible anymore, and these words are labeled archaic. However, to say that because of an archaic word here and there, that the KJB should be replaced with a modern version is nonsense. The Bible is the very words of God and is supposed to stand apart from the other books of this world. The English in the KJB is unique and can only be called Bible English. In 1611, when the KJB was first published, the people on the streets of London did not speak the same way the KJB speaks. The Bible is not supposed to sound like the common literature of the world, which is why the KJB is so unique in the way it sounds. It is God speaking, not men.

The truth is that today the KJB is the most read Bible in the United States. It is still the second best selling English version, behind the NIV. The fact that millions of people all over the world are reading the KJB everyday means that there are not any archaic words in it, because those words are still in common use by millions of people. I do not believe we should be changing the Bible to sound like the world, but rather the opposite is true.

There are deceivers that claim the KJB is too difficult for common people to understand. This is something I can refute from my own personal experience. When I was growing up, I did not like to read. I enjoyed playing sports much more. I was not a skilled reader and probably below average. However, when I was 32 years old, I started reading the KJB every day and believing it to be the pure words of God. Without help from anyone but God, I learned to read and understand the KJB very well. I have had Bible studies with a 9 year old little girl, and she was able to learn from and understand the KJB very well too. When there was something she did not understand she let me know, and I taught her the meaning. The KJB does an amazing job of defining difficult words in the context, and using a dictionary occasionally is not the end of the world. It is not the words in the Bible that are difficult for people to understand, but rather it is the deep spiritual concepts, that people struggle to grasp.

(1 Corinthians 2:13-14) 13 Which things also we speak, not in the words which man's wisdom teacheth, but which the Holy Ghost teacheth; comparing spiritual things with spiritual.

14 But the natural man receiveth not the things of the Spirit of God: for they are foolishness unto him: neither can he know them, because they are spiritually discerned.

THE GIFT OF ETERNAL LIFE

Before we move forward with identifying the King James Bible as God's pure words in English, we must deal with the most important issue first. The most important issue in the world for every person is the fact, that we are dead in sins until we receive the salvation of God by faith. The salvation of God means being saved from everlasting torment in hell fire and receiving forgiveness of our sins and the gift of eternal life in heaven. We will take the time here to present the gospel of our salvation with great clarity. If you are already saved that is great. However, someone who reads this book might still be lost and for the sake of that precious soul, we will explain very clearly how to receive eternal life.

The word "gospel" in the Bible means good news from God. However, before we can truly appreciate the good news, we must first understand the bad news. These next verses make it clear everybody has sinned.

(Romans 3:23) 23 For all have sinned, and come short of the glory of God;

(Romans 5:12) 12 Wherefore, as by one man sin entered into the world, and death by sin; and so death passed upon all men, for that all have sinned:

This next verse tells us because of our sin we deserve the wages of sin, which is death. This is more than a quick physical death, but rather an eternal death in the lake of fire. In Revelation 20:10-15, we see where all lost sinners will spend eternity.

3

(Romans 6:23) 23 For the wages of sin is death; but the gift of God is eternal life through Jesus Christ our Lord.

(Revelation 20:10-15) 10 And the devil that deceived them was cast into the lake of fire and brimstone, where the beast and the false prophet are, and shall be tormented day and night for ever and ever.

11 And I saw a great white throne, and him that sat on it, from whose face the earth and the heaven fled away; and there was found no place for them.

12 And I saw the dead, small and great, stand before God; and the books were opened: and another book was opened, which is the book of life: and the dead were judged out of those things which were written in the books, according to their works.

13 And the sea gave up the dead which were in it; and death and hell delivered up the dead which were in them: and they were judged every man according to their works.

14 And death and hell were cast into the lake of fire. This is the second death.

15 And whosoever was not found written in the book of life was cast into the lake of fire.

The devil and all lost sinners will be cast into the lake of fire and suffer eternal torment. This is extremely terrifying. However, Romans 6:23, tells us that the gift of God is eternal life, which is very good news. In Romans 1:16, we are told we receive this great salvation from God by believing the gospel of Christ.

(Romans 1:16) 16 For I am not ashamed of the gospel of Christ: for it is the power of God unto salvation to every one that believeth; to the Jew first, and also to the Greek.

The gospel of Christ that we must believe to receive forgiveness of sins, and the gift of eternal life, is plainly declared in 1 Corinthians 15:1-4. Verses 3 and 4 tell us specifically the gospel of our salvation.

(1 Corinthians 15:1-4) 1 Moreover, brethren, I declare unto you the gospel which I preached unto you, which also ye have received, and wherein ye stand;

2 By which also ye are saved, if ye keep in memory what I preached unto you, unless ye have believed in vain.

3 For I delivered unto you first of all that which I also received, how that Christ died for our sins according to the scriptures;

4 And that he was buried, and that he rose again the third day according to the scriptures:

Romans 1:16, tells us this gospel is the power of God unto salvation to everyone that believeth. In 1 Corinthians 15:2, it tells us this is the gospel by which we are saved. However, it says we are saved only if we keep it in memory, unless we have believed in vain. To keep the gospel in memory means we are not saved just because we have herd the gospel, but we need to know in our mind what the gospel is. Next it says, unless ye have believed in vain. To believe in vain means to believe for no purpose. So, we need to know what this gospel is, and for what purpose we are believing it. We are believing the gospel ("how that Christ died for our sins and was buried and rose again the third day") to receive forgiveness of sins and the gift of eternal life. This is the purpose for which we believe the gospel of Christ. How does a person believe in vain? If a person is trusting anything more than this gospel alone to be saved, then they are believing in vain. Examples would be, if a person says they believe the gospel and at the same time believe they also need to be water baptized, keep sacraments, or do good works to be saved, they are believing in vain. The person that believes in vain is not trusting Christ alone as Saviour. 1Corinthians 15:2 is saying, we need to know what we believe and why we believe it.

In 1Corinthians 15 verses 3 and 4, the Bible tells us the gospel we believe to be saved is, "how that Christ died for our sins, was buried, and rose again the third day." Notice it says "how" Christ died for our sins. He did not die of old age, but rather he shed blood and died on the cross for our sins. This made the atonement and paid the full price of redemption for the sins of all mankind. Notice it says "Christ," this is not the Lord's last name, but rather it is a title that declares Jesus is the Son of God our Saviour. In verse 4, the Bible declares after he died for our sins he rose from the dead the third day. The only way a person can receive eternal life today, is by believing this gospel alone to be saved. The gospel of our salvation is that Jesus, the Son of God, shed his blood and died on the cross for our sins, was buried, and rose again the third day.

After we believe this gospel alone to be saved, we receive eternal life and can never lose it under any circumstances. These next verses tell us after we believe the gospel of our salvation, that God seals us with his holy Spirit unto the day of redemption. Meaning we are eternally secure, or once saved always saved. Included in the following verses are other verses about our salvation in Christ.

(Ephesians 1:13) 13 In whom ye also trusted, after that ye heard the word of truth, the gospel of your salvation: in whom also after that ye believed, ye were sealed with that holy Spirit of promise,

(Ephesians 4:30) 30 And grieve not the holy Spirit of God, whereby ye are sealed unto the day of redemption.

(Ephesians 2:8-9) 8 For by grace are ye saved through faith; and that not of yourselves: it is the gift of God:

9 Not of works, lest any man should boast.

(1 Corinthians 1:17-18) 17 For Christ sent me not to baptize, but to preach the gospel: not with wisdom of words, lest the cross of Christ should be made of none effect.

18 For the preaching of the cross is to them that perish foolishness; but unto us which are saved it is the power of God.

(Romans 4:5) 5 But to him that worketh not, but believeth on him that justifieth the ungodly, his faith is counted for righteousness.

(Romans 5:1) 1 Therefore being justified by faith, we have peace with God through our Lord Jesus Christ:

(Ephesians 1:7) 7 In whom we have redemption through his blood, the forgiveness of sins, according to the riches of his grace;

(Romans 4:25) 25 Who was delivered for our offences, and was raised again for our justification.

(Colossians 2:9-10) 9 For in him dwelleth all the fulness of the Godhead bodily.

10 And ye are complete in him, which is the head of all principality and power:

Pure WORDS

8

A SHORT STORY

My grandpa Carl Drake loved the Lord and the word of God. He read the Bible from Genesis through Revelation many times. When I was in elementary school, sometimes I would spend a weekend with my grandpa and grandma, and they would take me to church with them. When I was 10 years old, I became very convicted of my sin and understood that if I did not receive salvation from God, that I would eventually die and go to hell. In tears, I called my grandpa and asked him how to be saved from going to hell. He told me to believe that Jesus Christ the Son of God died on the cross for my sins and rose from the dead. He told me that if I believed that in my heart, I would go to heaven.

Shortly after that, I went to visit him and I had a Bible with me, which my great aunt had given me. He showed me some verses about salvation and had me put a dot next to them, so it would be easy for me to find them. However, the first thing he did was check to see if it was an Authorized King James Bible. When he confirmed it was in fact a King James Bible, he told me very sincerely, that the King James Bible is the true words of God. He also told me that any other version including the New King James Bible had problems. My grandpa told me to make sure I only use the Authorized King James Bible.

I began going to church with my grandparents every Sunday for a couple months. Eventually summer came and my focus turned to baseball and going to the swimming pool. I got out of the routine of going to church. Well, when I was 32 years old, my grandpa died. As I was attending his funeral, the same preacher from when I was 10 years old was reading some verses from the KJB. Those words rang in my ears in a way that I cannot quite describe. I knew I was hearing real truth, and those words went straight through my ears into my heart. After the funeral, I went and found my old Bible, which had been collecting dust for many years. I began reading the Bible every day. I started watching some of the famous preachers on television and I noticed very few were using the King James Bible. After a couple years of Bible study and spiritual growth, I became so convinced in my heart that the KJB was in fact what my grandpa told me it was. The true words of God. I could not understand why so many famous preachers were using modern versions. I decided to study the Bible version issue myself, and the rest of this book will be dedicated to revealing what I learned.

(Hebrews 4:12) 12 For the word of God is quick, and powerful, and sharper than any twoedged sword, piercing even to the dividing asunder of soul and spirit, and of the joints and marrow, and is a discerner of the thoughts and intents of the heart.

BE A BIBLE BELIEVER

(1 Thessalonians 2:13) 13 For this cause also thank we God without ceasing, because, when ye received the word of God which ye heard of us, ye received it not as the word of men, but as it is in truth, the word of God, which effectually worketh also in you that believe.

Being a Bible believer means that we believe the words in the Bible that we hold in our hand are the very words God inspired and preserved for us. It means we take the words in the Bible we read as the absolute final authority over everything else in this world, including our favorite preacher.

Many call themselves Bible believers, but when they read something in the Bible that contradicts their personal belief system, they will go to other versions, or Hebrew and Greek lexicons, to choose a translation they prefer. This person's final authority is not one Bible they can hold in their hand, but rather their own opinion is their final authority. When we as Bible believers come to a verse that does not line up with our personal belief system, we change our belief system to match the Bible. We let the Bible correct us and avoid preachers that foolishly correct the Bible. We look to other Bible believers for edification. When we read something in the Bible we do not understand, we know the problem is with our understanding, not the Bible.

The thing the Bible version issue really comes down to is final authority. As a King James Bible believer, I take the words of the Bible I hold in my hand as the highest authority on earth. Anyone that thinks it is just fine to go back and forth between versions, or to correct the English using a Greek lexicon, makes themselves to be the final authority, rather than the words in one God inspired perfect book. When the Bible is our final authority the words in the Bible change us. When a person makes their own opinion the final authority, they end up changing the Bible. If a preacher cannot hold up one book and declare the book in their hand contains every pure word of God, then they are not qualified to preach. You will only learn to be a Bible believer from a Bible believer. Be careful who you listen to, brothers and sisters in Christ.

(Luke 4:4) 4 And Jesus answered him, saying, It is written, That man shall not live by bread alone, but by every word of God.

BEWARE OF THE WORLD'S WISDOM

(1Corinthians 3:19) 19 For the wisdom of this world is foolishness with God. For it is written, He taketh the wise in their own craftiness.

The Old Testament of the Bible was originally written in Hebrew with a small amount of Aramaic during a 1,000-year or more period of time. The New Testament was written in Koine Greek during the 1st century A.D. The Bible was progressively written over a time spanning over 1,400 years and there are believed to be 40 different penmen. Today, we have not one single original manuscript available. The major battle in our time is over the text of the New Testament, so that is what this book will address. A manuscript is simply a handwritten document. The printing press was not available until the mid-1400's A.D. It is claimed that today we have over 5,800 New Testament Greek manuscripts, and some of these being just fragments.

We have no need for original manuscripts, because the Bible tells us in verses such as Psalm 12:6,7 and Matthew 24:35, that God has promised to preserve his words forever. In the book of Jeremiah chapter 36, we read about an original manuscript inspired by God, burned up in a fire. The Bible tells us after this had happened, there was another copy written that contained all the words of the original, also we are told there were added besides unto these words many like words. The Bible is God's book, and he will preserve it however which way he chooses. This chapter in Jeremiah tells us the second copy of the original manuscript was not identical to the first, however both were given by inspiration of God. God does not play by the rules that textual critics make up.

(1 Timothy 6:20-21) 20 O Timothy, keep that which is committed to thy trust, avoiding profane and vain babblings, and oppositions of science falsely so called:

21 Which some professing have erred concerning the faith. Grace be with thee. Amen.

Textual Criticism is the science that seeks to reconstruct the original text of scripture based on existing manuscripts. So, to be a textual critic, a person must believe that no one today has a copy of God's pure and perfect words. Textual critics reject what the Bible teaches about the words of God being preserved. These people are not Bible believers, but rather they are deceivers that work for the devil. These men tell us no one today can hold a copy of God's pure words in their hand. These are highly educated infidels who have no final authority other than their own opinions. We are told that they are in the process of figuring out what the Bible should really say, and we should trust them.

Starting in the mid-1800's, two textual critics with the last names Westcott and Hort created their own Greek New Testament, which today is called the *Critical Greek Text*. The pure text of the New Testament, which has been in constant use by Bible believers since the 1st century is called, the *Received Greek Text*. We will talk about these two different Greek New Testaments in this book. However, I wanted to take the time to explain what a textual critic is. If these people confessed that God preserved his words, then they would be out of a job and a paycheck. *Modern Textual Criticism* is evil, because it rejects what God has said about preserving his words and tells us that we cannot have a copy of God's pure words. I know I am using strong language, but this needs to be said. These men are full of the wisdom of this world and want us to trust them more than the Bible in our hand.

(1Corinthians 3:19-20) 19 For the wisdom of this world is foolishness with God. For it is written, He taketh the wise in their own craftiness.

20 And again, The Lord knoweth the thoughts of the wise, that they are vain.

(1Cornthians 2:5) 5 That your faith should not stand in the wisdom of men, but in the power of God.

Pure WORDS

16

THE RECEIVED GREEK TEXT

(Psalm 12:6-7) 6 The words of the LORD are pure words: as silver tried in a furnace of earth, purified seven times.

7 Thou shalt keep them, O LORD, thou shalt preserve them from this generation for ever.

(Isaiah 40:8) 8 The grass withereth, the flower fadeth: but the word of our God shall stand for ever.

We will take a brief look at the history of the text of the New Testament. The above Bible verses declare that God's words are pure, and that he will keep and preserve them forever. God has promised us his pure words will always be available, so it is our job to identify and use those pure words. In 2Corinthians 2:17, the apostle Paul declares that many were corrupting the word of God during the 1st century. From the 1st century until today there have been two lines of textual transmission. There has been a pure line and a corrupt line of textual transmission from the time of the apostle Paul until today.

The printing press was invented during the mid- 1400's, and this was an important time for the transmission and preservation of the Bible. In the early 1500's, a brilliant Latin and Greek scholar by the last name Erasmus, was working on getting the New Testament in the original Greek language into print. He spent years journeying all over Europe visiting libraries and anyone from whom he could get manuscript readings. Erasmus when speaking about his work on the New Testament is quoted as saying, "If I told what sweat it cost me, no one would believe me." He printed five editions of the New Testament in Greek; the last one was printed in 1535. This Greek text was later refined and printed by others. The most prominent editions are the 1551 edition by Robert Estienne, better known as the Latinized Robert Stephanus, which added the verse divisions we use today, and the 1598 edition by Theodore Beza, which is the edition more than likely in the hands of the King James Bible translators. However, the KJB translators had access to all editions, which are all the same text with minor refinements.

This Greek text was later named the "*Textus Receptus*," which is Latin for "*Received Text.*" This text is also called the *Traditional, Majority,* or the *Byzantine Text.* There are over 5,800 Greek New Testament manuscripts available today, and 99% support this *Received Text.* More than 90% of all the Greek manuscripts are in very strong cohesive agreement with each other. One of, if not the oldest available manuscript, that textual critics have named P-66 is dated around A.D. 125, it contains most of the book of John and supports the *Received Text.* The old Latin and Syriac translations, which date back to A.D. 150, support the *Received Text.* This *Received Text* is the New Testament that was passed from Bible believer to Bible believer from the 1st century until today. This is the pure line of transmission, and this is the text that has been in constant use by Christians, for close to 2,000 years. This is the text the King James Bible translators used for the New Testament.

(Psalm 119:140) 140 Thy word is very pure: therefore thy servant loveth it.

THE CRITICAL GREEK TEXT

(2Corinthians 2:17) 17 For we are not as many, which corrupt the word of God: but as of sincerity, but as of God, in the sight of God speak we in Christ.

The current Greek text from which modern Bible version New Testaments are translated is called the *Critical Greek Text*. It is also referred to as the *Nestle-Aland* and *UBS text*. This *Critical Greek Text* was first published in 1881. This text was created and edited by two textual critics by the last names Westcott and Hort. These men in their own writings claim not to believe in the divine inspiration of the holy scriptures. They also did not believe in the Genesis account of creation, but rather supported Darwinian evolution. They did not believe Jesus Christ's blood sacrifice on the cross made the atonement for the sins of all mankind. What has just been said about these men comes from their own writings.

The new *Critical Greek Text* that these men produced was based almost 100% on only two of the more than 5,800 available manuscripts. These two manuscripts are called *Vaticanus* and *Sinaiticus*. The main reason textual critics place so much authority on these two manuscripts is because it is claimed they are very old, and they both contain most of the New Testament. It is claimed these two manuscripts date back to around A.D. 350. The other manuscripts of that age are mostly fragments, but these two are almost complete New Testaments. So, because of the supposed old age of these two manuscripts, textual critics ignore the thousands of other manuscripts and focus on primarily these two.

Westcott and Hort blended these two manuscripts to create the modern *Critical Text*. These manuscripts are commonly referred to as the oldest and best manuscripts.

The fact is that these two manuscripts might be old, but they are demonstrably corrupt and should never be used for translation. The documented fact is that *Vaticanus* and *Sinaiticus* disagree with each other in over 3,000 places in the books Matthew, Mark, Luke, and John, alone. *Sinaiticus* has many alterations, which revert readings to match the *Received Text*. The *Received Text* can be traced back to A.D. 150 in manuscript P-66, the old Latin, and Syriac translation. The *Received Text* is proven to be well over 100 years older than *Vaticanus* and *Sinaiticus*. The *Received Text* has been in continual use by the professing Christian church for almost 2,000 years. *Vaticanus* and *Sinaiticus* sat around on a shelf and were ignored because they are corrupt and full of errors and omissions. Whereas the *Received Text* was in constant use being worn out and recopied repeatedly. Think about how much effort it takes to hand write the whole New Testament. Do you not think the scribes in those days would have more knowledge of the correct text than textual critics more than 1,000 years later? There have never been any copies of *Vaticanus* or *Sinaiticus* found. This is because they are corrupt, and no one used them.

Many today are challenging the age of these two manuscripts, with what seems to be convincing evidence they were produced after A.D. 1400. This would mean they are 1,000 years younger than many have thought. Weather they are old or not does not really matter, rather what matters is that they are corrupt and water down major Bible doctrines. Remember what the apostle Paul said in the 1st century. People corrupting the word of God is nothing new.

(2Corinthians 2:17) 17 For we are not as many, which corrupt the word of God: but as of sincerity, but as of God, in the sight of God speak we in Christ.

THE MANUSCRIPTS

Of the more than 5,800 New Testament Greek manuscripts, over 90% are in strong cohesive agreement with each other. This group represents the *Received Text*, which Erasmus put into print in the early 1500's. This is the text used by the translators of the King James Bible. Of the more than 5,800 available Greek manuscripts, less than 1% support the modern Critical Text. Around 97% of the modern *Critical Text* is based on only two manuscripts, *Vaticanus* and *Sinaiticus*. This is the text used to translate modern versions such as the NIV, ESV, NASB, NLT, NRSV, and many more. So less than 1% of the manuscripts support the New Testament in the modern versions. The *Received Text* contains 140,523 words and the *Critical Text* contains 137,976 words, so the *Critical Text* contains 2,547 less words than the *Received Text*. These missing words effect major Bible doctrines, and we will show this when we do a brief comparison between modern versions and the KJB.

If we look at the big picture and divide all the manuscripts according to which text they support, we find staggering results. Of the available Greek manuscripts of the New Testament, 99% support the *Received Text* over the *Critical Text*, and less than 1% of these manuscripts support the *Critical Text* over the *Received Text*. The modern *Critical Text* is a man-made corrupt text, which makes modern versions that are translated from it corrupt as well. The *Received Text* is the Bible that has been in constant use and passed down by Bible believers century after century. The *Received Text* is the preserved words of God in Greek, and the King James Bible is the preserved words of God in English.

Most of the so-called textual scholars make up rules and theories that they expect others to buy into. They use sophisticated terminology and talk in ways most people simply do not understand. They have intimidated many professing Christians into looking to them as the final authority concerning the text of the Bible. The modern *Critical Text* they created is still evolving, and is currently on its 28th edition, since 1881. The textual critics do not believe God has preserved a pure text, rather they believe they are in the process of restoring the text to what it should say according to their own opinion.

The truth is that God does not operate according to what these so-called scholars say or think. He is not forced to play by their rules. We will never understand every detail about how God has preserved his words. When we believe what the Bible says about itself, and then study the details about the history of the text, we can then identify the *Received Text* as the pure line of textual transmission. The final purified crown jewel of the pure text in English is the King James Bible.

(Psalm 119:128-130) 128 Therefore I esteem all thy precepts concerning all things to be right; and I hate every false way.

129 Thy testimonies are wonderful: therefore doth my soul keep them.

130 The entrance of thy words giveth light; it giveth understanding unto the simple.

THE HISTORY
OF THE KJB

In 1526, a brave and brilliant man who was fluent in seven languages, was able to print his translation of the New Testament into modern English. This man's name was William Tyndale, and he was the first person to translate the *Received Greek Text* into modern English. During the process of this work, Tyndale understood that if the Roman Catholic church caught him, they would charge him as a heretic and put him to death. The Catholic church at that time did not want the common people to have the Bible in their own language, because they did not want anyone questioning the authority of the church. They had the Bible in Latin, since around A.D. 400, and preferred to keep it that way because by the 1500's few people could read Latin. Even though Tyndale was facing the death penalty if he got caught, he was willing to put his life on the line to get the words of God to the common people. The Roman Catholic church back then and today teach many unbiblical doctrines that are the tradition of men, and not Bible truths. Many were burned to death at the stake for preaching against the false doctrines of the Catholic church. They were after Tyndale and hunted him like an animal. They finally caught him, and on October 6, 1536, William Tyndale was chained to a stake and strangled to death by an executioner, and his body was set on fire.

The first complete Bible containing the Old and New Testaments in modern English, appeared in 1535, and was the work of Miles Coverdale. His work was followed by the Matthews Bible in 1537, which was the work of a man named John Rogers. Rogers was captured by the Roman Catholic authorities and publicly burned to death in 1555. The next English Bibles in the purified line that led to the King James Bible were the Great Bible 1539, the Geneva Bible 1560, and the Bishops Bible in A.D. 1568. The English Bible was going through a purification process that would come to completion with the rubbed and polished crown jewel being the King James Bible in A.D. 1611.

Throughout the 1500's, and early 1600's, the study and understanding of biblical Hebrew, Greek, and Latin was very intense. The scholars of those days studied the biblical languages from the time they were young children. At the universities of Cambridge and Oxford in the early 1600's, theology was the chief subject. At this time scholarship concerning the biblical languages was at its pinnacle. Biblical scholars today are not close to the knowledge and understanding of the men chosen to translate the King James Bible. God preserves his words, and he had the right men at the right time to give the world a perfect Bible in English.

In 1604, King James 1 of England appointed 54 of the finest biblical scholars in the world to bring to pass a new translation of the holy scriptures into the English language. Though we know 54 men were selected, most of the old lists have the names of 47 men. One of the translators named John Bois, could read the complete Old Testament in the Hebrew language when he was just 5 years old. He was a legitimate Greek scholar at the age of 14. Another of the translators named John Rainolds, was thought to have died early by too intense application to study. When he was urged to ease up on his labors, he replied, for the sake of life, he would not lose the very end of living. These men lived in a world far different than the world we live in today. These men reached a level of scholarship that far exceeds today's modern textual critics. These men were God fearing men, that truly believed they were handling the very words of God. Though they were some of the most learned men to ever live, they were humble and worked as a team.

In the Bible's preface called, "The Translators to the reader," they say, "to that purpose there were many chosen that were greater in other men's eyes than their own, and that sought the truth rather than their own praise." In the conclusion of their preface they say, "It is a fearful thing to fall into the hands of the living God; but a blessed thing it is, and will bring us to everlasting blessedness in the end, when God speaketh unto us, to hearken; when he setteth his word before us, to read it; when he strecheth out his hand and calleth, to answer, Here am I, here we are to do thy will, O God. The Lord work a care and conscience in us to know him and serve him, that we may be acknowledged of him at the appearing of our Lord JESUS CHRIST, to whom with the Holy Ghost be all praise and thanksgiving. Amen."

The translators were divided into six companies, two at Cambridge, two at Oxford, and two at Westminster. For seven years (1604-1611) the translators diligently worked to produce a standard English Bible. In their preface they say, "Truly, good Christian Reader, we never thought from the beginning that we should need to make a new translation, nor yet to make of a bad one a good one . . . but to make a good one better, or out of many good ones one principal good one, not justly to be excepted against; that hath been our endeavour, that our mark." By the process in which they used, every word in the Bible was examined at least 14 times by each translator. In A.D. 1611 the King James Bible was published. The exact number is only known to God, but from 1611 until today there have been billions of King James Bibles printed. Since 1611, there have been four major editions of the KJB. The first two editions were produced in 1629 and 1638. Printing in those days was a difficult task, and with a huge book like the Bible, some printing errors were unavoidable. The editions of 1629 and 1638 were to correct minor printing errors. Two of the original translators, John Bois and Samuel Ward, worked on the 1638 edition and it stood as the standard for well over 100 years. The two final editions were published in 1762 and 1769. In 1611, English spelling and punctuation had not yet been standardized.

The 1762 and 1769 editions fully modernized and standardized the spelling and punctuation of the King James Bible. The edition we use today is the 1769 edition.

The 1611 King James Bible and the KJB we use today are the same book. Apart from the correcting of printer errors and updating spelling and punctuation, remains very little word variation between the 1611 edition and the edition we use today. Here are some examples of the very minor word variations that do exist.

(Luke 23:19) 19 (Who for a certain sedition made in the city, and for murder, was cast into prison.)

(Luke 23:19-1611 edition) Who for a certaine sedition made in the citie, and for murder, was cast in prison.

The current edition says, "was cast into prison."

The 1611 edition says, "was cast in prison." The word "in" was changed to "into."

(James 5:4) 4 Behold, the hire of the labourers who have reaped down your fields, which is of you kept back by fraud, crieth: and the cries of them which have reaped are entered into the ears of the Lord of sabaoth.

(James 5:4-1611 edition) Beholde, the hire of the labourers which have reaped downe your fieldes, which is of you kept backe by fraud, cryeth : and the cryes of them which have reaped, are entered into the eares of the Lord of Sabaoth.

The current edition says, "the hire of the labourers who have reaped down your fields"

The 1611 edition says, "the hire of the labourers which have reaped downe your fieldes"

The word "which" was changed to "who."

These variations are rare and simply part of the refining process that brought the KJB to its perfected final form that we use today. The 1611

KJB and the KJB we use today are the same book. As we look back at some of the details in the history of the English Bible, we see men of great courage and skill translating and refining our perfect English Bible. However, our faith is not in the wisdom of men, but rather in the power of God. Though we take some comfort in the fact that God used men of such great knowledge and skill to give us his pure words in English, our faith is in God, to perform, and preserve his words just as the Bible declares. The key is to believe what the Bible says about itself.

(Psalm 12:6-7) 6 The words of the LORD are pure words: as silver tried in a furnace of earth, purified seven times.

7 Thou shalt keep them, O LORD, thou shalt preserve them from this generation for ever.

(Isaiah 40:8) 8 The grass withereth, the flower fadeth: but the word of our God shall stand for ever.

(Matthew 24:35) 35 Heaven and earth shall pass away, but my words shall not pass away.

Pure WORDS

INSPIRATION AND THE KJB

When we read statements of faith, which have been prepared by Christian denominations and Bible colleges concerning what they believe about the inspiration of God and the scriptures, we will notice something most of them have in common. They say that they believe God inspired the original autographs, but nothing about us having an inspired Bible today. When asked if we can hold an inspired Bible in our hand today, almost all of them say, no. This mentality comes from the modern textual critics, not from the Bible. However, God does not play by the rules the scholars make up. If we really want to know what is given by inspiration of God, then we must search the scriptures for the answer.

(2 Timothy 3:15-16) 15 And that from a child thou hast known the holy scriptures, which are able to make thee wise unto salvation through faith which is in Christ Jesus.

16 All scripture is given by inspiration of God, and is profitable for doctrine, for reproof, for correction, for instruction in righteousness:

In verse 15, Paul says that Timothy from the time he was a child, knew the holy scriptures, which at that time was the Old Testament. Moses wrote the first five books of the Bible over a thousand years before Timothy was born, and most of the other books were written well over 500 years before Timothy was born. Nothing Timothy had access to as a child was an original autograph. After calling what Timothy had as a child, holy scriptures, Paul then in verse 16 says that all scripture is given by inspiration of God. This then, identifies the copies that Timothy had from a child as God inspired words. According to what the Bible tells us, an accurate copy of the original is just as inspired as the original. So, if the King James Bible is an accurate copy of the holy scriptures, and it is, then this means the KJB is in fact the inspired and preserved words of God.

Keeping in mind that 2Timothy 3:16 says, all scripture is given by inspiration of God. Now, when we read Luke 4:16-19, the Bible tells us the Lord Jesus is in a synagogue in Nazareth and reads from the book of Isaiah. Two verses later in Luke 4:21, Christ calls what he just read, scripture. This means at that synagogue they had an inspired copy of Isaiah. In Acts 8:27,28 it says the Ethiopian eunuch sitting in his chariot was reading Isaiah, then verse 32 calls what he was reading, scripture. This means it was the inspired words of God. The scholars tell us only the original autographs can be inspired words of God. If this was true, that would mean in Luke chapter 4 they had an original copy of Isaiah. This would mean the eunuch in Acts chapter 8, somehow obtained that exact copy of Isaiah for himself. Of course these are two separate copies of Isaiah, and the Bible calls them both scripture. 2Timothy 3:16 says, all scripture is given by inspiration of God, and the Bible identifies both copies of Isaiah as scripture. This means accurate copies are the inspired words of God.

The Bible colleges, scholars, and most preachers will tell us, only the original autographs are the inspired words of God, and we cannot hold an inspired Bible in our hand today. The Bible tells us accurate copies are the inspired words of God. This means if the Bible we hold in our hand is an accurate copy of the scriptures, then we are holding the inspired words of God in our hand. Moreover, in Acts chapter 22, we are told that Paul was speaking to the Jews in Hebrew, well the writer of Acts recorded it in Greek. This tells us that God has no problem inspiring translations. The King James Bible in English and any Bible in any language that is an accurate copy of the scriptures, is the inspired words of God. Do not ever be intimidated by the scholars or academia. Make the Bible your final authority and your faith and confidence in the Bible will increase greatly.

(Psalm 138:2) 2 I will worship toward thy holy temple, and praise thy name for thy lovingkindness and for thy truth: <u>for thou hast magnified thy word above all thy name.</u>

Pure WORDS

COMPARING THE KJB WITH MODERN VERSIONS

Almost every modern English Bible version available is translated from the corrupt *Critical Greek Text*. Therefore, the modern English Bibles are corrupt as well. The *Critical Text* has over 2,500 less words than the God preserved *Received Text*, and what is missing has a major effect on important doctrines. The *New International Version* (NIV) is probably the most popular of the modern versions so we will use it for an example, but all modern versions translated from the *Critical Text* have this same corruption. When compared to the New Testament of the KJB, the NIV says "God" 31 less times, "Jesus" 36 less times, "Christ" 44 less times, and "Lord" 35 less times. This fact alone shows us something is terribly wrong with the modern English Bibles.

In the following, we will look at a verse from the KJB in bold and the same verse from the NIV in Italic font. I will make brief comments on the comparison. We will only look at a few verses, so this is just a small sample of the problem with modern versions.

(1 Timothy 3:16) 16 And without controversy great is the mystery of godliness: <u>God</u> was manifest in the flesh, justified in the Spirit, seen of angels, preached unto the Gentiles, believed on in the world, received up into glory.

(1 Timothy 3:16 NIV) 16 Beyond all question, the mystery from which true godliness springs is great: <u>He</u> appeared in the flesh, was vindicated by the Spirit, was seen by angels, was preached among the nations, was believed on in the world, was taken up in glory.

33

Look at what is underlined in these verses. The KJB makes it clear that Jesus Christ was God manifest in the flesh and the NIV simply says He appeared in the flesh. The KJB exalts Christ and the NIV does not.

(Ephesians 3:9) 9 And to make all men see what is the fellowship of the mystery, which from the beginning of the world hath been hid in God, who created all things <u>by Jesus Christ:</u>

(Ephesians 3:9 NIV) 9 and to make plain to everyone the administration of this mystery, which for ages past was kept hidden in God, who created all things.

The KJB tells us Jesus Christ created everything and the NIV completely removes the name of our Saviour from the verse.

(Colossians 1:14) 14 In whom we have redemption through his <u>blood,</u> even the forgiveness of sins:

(Colossians 1:14 NIV) 14 in whom we have redemption, the forgiveness of sins.

In the KJB, we see the importance of the blood of Christ in this verse and the NIV completely removes the blood in this verse.

(Luke 4:4) 4 And Jesus answered him, saying, It is written, That man shall not live by bread alone, but <u>by every word of God.</u>

(Luke 4:4 NIV) 4 Jesus answered, "It is written: 'Man shall not live on bread alone.'"

The KJB tells us we need every word of God, and the NIV completely removes these words.

(Matthew 18:11) 11 For the Son of man is come to save that which was lost.

(Matthew 18:11 NIV) 11

The NIV and most modern versions remove this important verse entirely, because it is not in the *Critical Greek Text*.

This has only been a very small sample of the corruption in modern versions. Many more examples can be given, but I think this is sufficient to show that, which Bible we use really does matter. The New King James Bible claims to be translated from the *Received Text*; however, it has many problems and should never be used in place of the real KJB. The New King James Version (NKJV), in the Old and New Testament omits "Lord" 66 times, "God" 51 times, "heaven" 50 times, "blood" 23 times, and "hell" 22 times. The pure English Bible is the King James Bible, do not be deceived.

(Proverbs 30:5) 5 Every word of God is pure: he is a shield unto them that put their trust in him.

Pure WORDS

CONCLUSION

History and manuscript evidence are helpful to identify the pure text. However, many of the manuscripts from the 1st century to the end of the 15th century are no longer in existence. Many centuries ago, around A.D. 303-312, the Roman emperor Diocletian tried to eradicate Christianity by searching out and destroying every copy of the scriptures he could find. Also, during the Roman Catholic Inquisition from just after 1200 A.D. to around A.D. 1750, the Catholic church murdered multitudes of innocent Christians for simply rejecting certain Roman Catholic doctrines. Not only were many Bible believing Christians put to death, but the manuscripts that belonged to these Christians were destroyed as well.

We will never understand every detail about how God has preserved his words. We can however be thankful the Lord has allowed enough information to be available, so that we can easily identify the pure text, and mark and avoid the corrupt text. We have not been left to rely on textual critics to tell us what God has said. These so-called scholars have rejected the Bible doctrine of preservation and believe they are in a continuing process of reconstructing the Bible to the original autographs, of which there is not one currently in existence. Their *Critical Greek Text* is in its 28th edition since 1881 and is still evolving. This is why the modern versions such as the NIV, ESV, and NASB are constantly being updated and changed. The truth is we have always had the pure text from the beginning. It has been in constant use by the true church, which is the body of Christ, from the first century until today.

Isaiah 46:10, declares that God knows the end from the beginning. In 1611, less than 3% of the world's population spoke English, and today English is the most widely known, used, and spoken language in the world. God, in his foreknowledge brought forth the King James Bible, knowing that the English language would become the dominate language on this earth. From the mid 1600's until the late 1800's, a time of over 250 years, the King James Bible was basically the only English Bible people used. The KJB was taken all over the world and brought forth much fruit, before the modern versions were created. The King James Bible is still the most read and second-best selling Bible, today. It is the English Bible that truly has God's stamp of approval. It is the standard Bible on earth today and has been for over 400 years. As long as English is a spoken language the King James Bible will be the final authority in English. It truly is the inspired and preserved words of God.

(Psalm 12:6-7) 6 The words of the LORD are pure words: as silver tried in a furnace of earth, purified seven times.

7 Thou shalt keep them, O LORD, thou shalt preserve them from this generation for ever.

(2Samuel 22:31) 31 As for God, his way is perfect; the word of the LORD is tried: he is a buckler to all them that trust in him.

(1Thessalonians 2:13) 13 For this cause also thank we God without ceasing, because, when ye received the word of God which ye heard of us, ye received it not as the word of men, but as it is in truth, the word of God, which effectually worketh also in you that believe.

APPENDIX

The Apocrypha

The Apocrypha is a collection of books that were not given by inspiration of God. These books are in the Old Testament of the Catholic Bible. The Coverdale Bible (1535), Matthews Bible (1537), Great Bible (1539), Geneva Bible (1560), Bishops Bible (1568), and the King James Bible (1611) contain these books in between the Old and New Testaments. *The Apocrypha* was inserted between the Testaments as supplemental historical reading. These books were never considered part of the holy scriptures by King James, or the translators of the Bibles previously mentioned. In the 1611 King James Bible, these books are labeled *"Apocrypha"* at the top of each page so they would not be confused with the scriptures. These books are labeled like this to clearly identify them as separate from the scriptures. On the title page of the 1611 KJB, it says "The Holy Bible containing the Old Testament and the New: Newly translated out of the Original tongues and with the former Translations diligently compared and revised, by his Majesties special commandment." We see they considered only the Old and New Testaments as the Holy Bible. Other than being supplemental historical reading, there is another major reason for its inclusion. In those days there were heated debates between Catholics and Protestants, and since these books were in the Catholic Old Testament, the Protestants needed to be familiar with those books. In the 1800's, the *Apocrypha* was removed from basically all King James Bibles. Around A.D. 100, the Jewish historian Josephus confirms that those books were not considered inspired scripture, even in his day.

Pure WORDS

BIBLIOGRAPHY

This is a short list of helpful books about the Bible version issue.

The History of Your Bible, Terence D. McLean

Which Translation Should You Trust? Timothy S. Morton

From the Original Texts to the English Bible, Timothy S. Morton

Study Notes on the King James Bible, David O'Steen

Missing in Modern Bibles, Jack A. Moorman

King James, His Bible, and its Translators, Third Edition, Laurence M. Vance

The Word: God will Keep It, Joey Faust

Which Version Is The Bible? Floyd Nolen Jones

Ripped out of the Bible, Floyd Nolen Jones

The Glorious History of the English Bible, David Cloud

The Faithful Word, David H. Sorenson

In Defense of the Authenticity of 1 John 5:7, Second Edition, C.H. Pappas

The Answer Book, Dr. Samuel C. Gipp

Crowned With Glory, Dr. Thomas Holland

Pure WORDS

42

ABOUT THE AUTHOR

Jeffery Drake, Jr. is a passionate advocate for the King James Bible as God's preserved word. Growing up in a family with deep respect for scripture, Jeffery's journey of faith led him to study the Bible in depth, finding clarity and conviction in the King James Bible. Through personal testimony and rigorous study, Jeffery has dedicated his life to encouraging believers to embrace the KJB as the ultimate authority. His experiences and insights have equipped him to address common misconceptions, making Pure Words a vital resource for Christians today.

Trust Publishers House,
the trusted name in quality Christian books.

Trust House Publishers
PO Box 3181
Taos, NM 87571

TrustHousePublishers.com

www.ingramcontent.com/pod-product-compliance
Lightning Source LLC
Chambersburg PA
CBHW061720120626
46550CB00003B/1306